U.S. HISTORY Need to Know

SilverTip

The Civil War

by Karen Latchana Kenney

Consultant: Caitlin Krieck
Social Studies Teacher and Instructional Coach
The Lab School of Washington

BEARPORT
PUBLISHING

Minneapolis, Minnesota

Credits

Cover and title page, © Currier and Ives/Wikimedia Creative Commons license 3.0; 5, © Archive Images/Alamy; 7, © Everett Collection/Shutterstock; 9, © ilbusca/Getty Images; 11, © Buyenlarge/Getty Images; 13, © Everett Collection/Shutterstock; 14, © Stocktrek Images, Inc./Alamy; 15, © Everett Collection Inc/Alamy; 16–17, © Classic Image/Alamy; 18–19, © LC-DIG-pga-01843/Library of Congress; 21, © LC-DIG-pga-08284/Library of Congress; 22–23, © LC-DIG-pga-02102/Library of Congress; 25, © Keith Lance/iStock; and 27, © The Protected Art Archive/Alamy.

Bearport Publishing Company Product Development Team

President: Jen Jenson; Director of Product Development: Spencer Brinker; Managing Editor: Allison Juda; Associate Editor: Naomi Reich; Associate Editor: Tiana Tran; Senior Designer: Colin O'Dea; Associate Designer: Elena Klinkner; Associate Designer: Kayla Eggert; Product Development Specialist: Anita Stasson

A NOTE FROM THE PUBLISHER: Some of the historic photos in this book have been colorized to help readers have a more meaningful and rich experience. The color results are not intended to depict actual historical detail.

Library of Congress Cataloging-in-Publication Data

Names: Kenney, Karen Latchana, author.
Title: The Civil War / by Karen Latchana Kenney.
Description: Silvertip books. | Minneapolis, Minnesota : Bearport
    Publishing Company, [2024] | Series: U.S. history: need to know |
    Includes bibliographical references and index.
Identifiers: LCCN 2023001673 (print) | LCCN 2023001674 (ebook) | ISBN
    9798888220290 (library binding) | ISBN 9798888222201 (paperback) | ISBN
    9798888223444 (ebook)
Subjects: LCSH: United States—History—Civil War, 1861-1865—Juvenile
    literature.
Classification: LCC E468 .K357 2024 (print) | LCC E468 (ebook) | DDC
    973.7—dc23/eng/20230113
LC record available at https://lccn.loc.gov/2023001673
LC ebook record available at https://lccn.loc.gov/2023001674

Copyright © 2024 Bearport Publishing Company. All rights reserved. No part of this publication may be reproduced in whole or in part, stored in any retrieval system, or transmitted in any form or by any means, electronic, mechanical, photocopying, recording, or otherwise, without written permission from the publisher.

For more information, write to Bearport Publishing, 5357 Penn Avenue South, Minneapolis, MN 55419.

Contents

Raging War 4

Freedom and Slavery 6

Two Sides 8

New President, New Country . . . 12

War Begins 16

Southern Victories. 18

Slavery Ends 20

Northern Gains 22

Trying to Unite 26

The Places of the Civil War 28

SilverTips for Success 29

Glossary 30

Read More. 31

Learn More Online. 31

Index 32

About the Author 32

Raging War

The crowd watched as President Abraham Lincoln stepped across the stage. He was in Gettysburg, Pennsylvania, to speak about the Civil War. Lincoln urged the people of the North to keep fighting. This war would change the country's future.

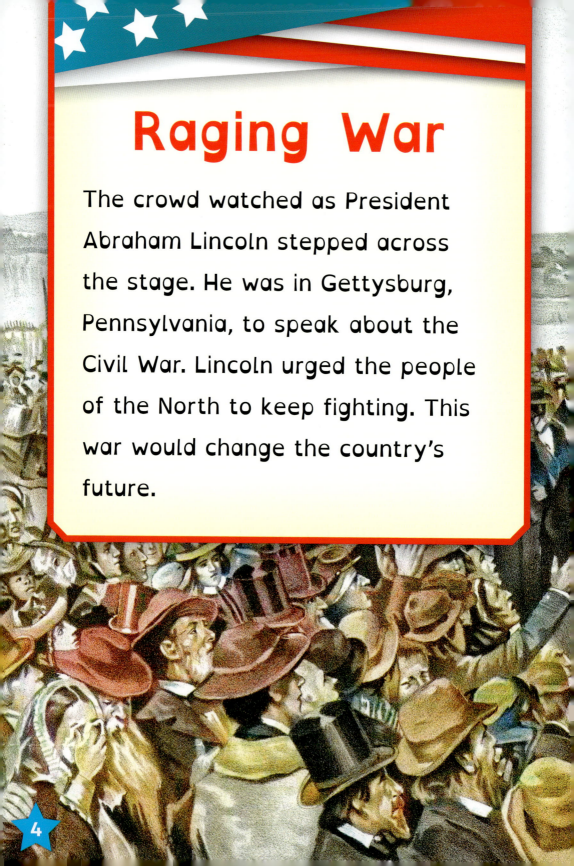

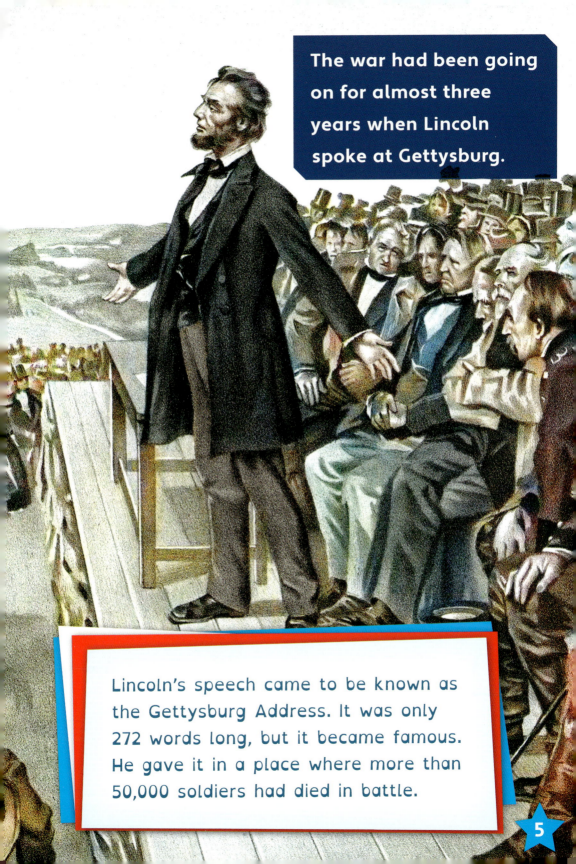

The war had been going on for almost three years when Lincoln spoke at Gettysburg.

Lincoln's speech came to be known as the Gettysburg Address. It was only 272 words long, but it became famous. He gave it in a place where more than 50,000 soldiers had died in battle.

Freedom and Slavery

The United States was formed with the idea of freedom. Yet, for a long time, many people were not truly free. Black people across the country were forced into **slavery**. Laws allowed White people to own Black people. These laws kept many people from having rights and freedom.

Many people forced into slavery were taken from Africa. By 1860, there were more than four million people who were enslaved in the United States.

Two Sides

People across the country had different ideas about slavery. In southern states, wealthy people made money by running large farms called **plantations**. They used enslaved workers on their farms. Many people in the South wanted slavery to stay.

Plantations often had hundreds of workers. They grew mostly cotton, rice, and tobacco. Some had corn or sugarcane. Farming these crops was difficult and painful work.

Cotton had to be picked by hand.

Northern states made much of their money in a different way. Many people worked in factories. There were big banks and newspapers, too. In the North, slavery became illegal over time. Some Northerners wanted slavery to be illegal in the whole country.

Slavery was not allowed in the North. However, there were Northerners who were involved in slavery. They had businesses that made money from the slave trade.

New President, New Country

By 1860, the country was divided about slavery. It was also facing a major election. The vote could change everything. Abraham Lincoln was running for president. He was against slavery. Southern states made a threat. If Lincoln won, they would **secede**. They said they would form a new country.

John Breckinridge was also running in the election. He was the choice for Southern states. Breckinridge supported slavery.

Lincoln won the election. Right away, seven states in the South seceded. The states left the United States. They formed a new country with its own government. It was called the **Confederate States of America**. The states in the North became known as the Union.

The Confederate States chose Jefferson Davis to be their president. He was born and raised in the South. His family owned a cotton plantation with enslaved people.

The Confederate states made their own flag.

War Begins

Soon after the Confederacy formed, tensions rose. The South wanted to control military forts in the land it claimed as its own. The Union would not allow it.

On April 12, 1861, Confederate soldiers attacked Fort Sumter in South Carolina. They soon took control. This was the start of the Civil War.

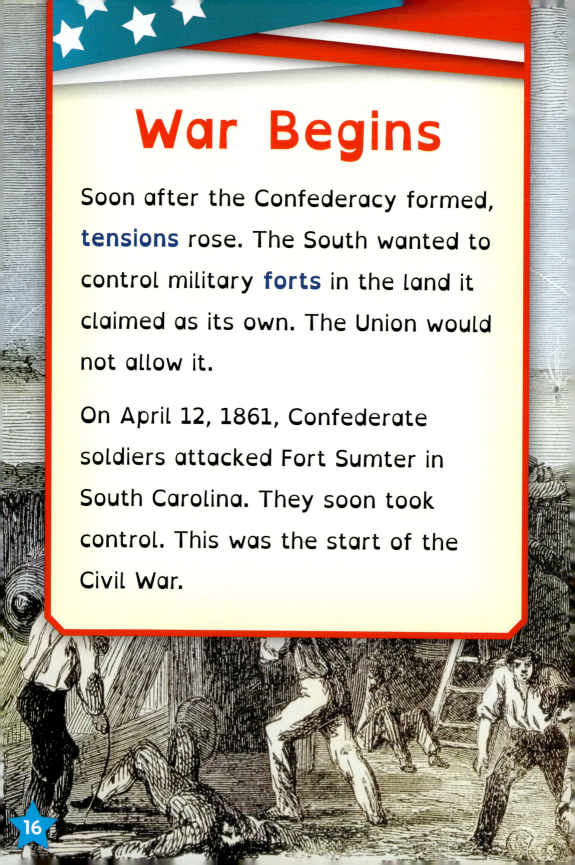

When the war started, both sides needed to get troops quickly. Many of the men who joined were not ready to fight. Most had little training. They had never been in the military before.

The attack on Fort Sumter

Southern Victories

The North had more guns, weapons, and people. They thought it would be a quick and easy fight. Yet, the South surprised them.

In **July 1861**, the South beat the North at the Battle of Bull Run. Early in the war, the South had more victories than the North.

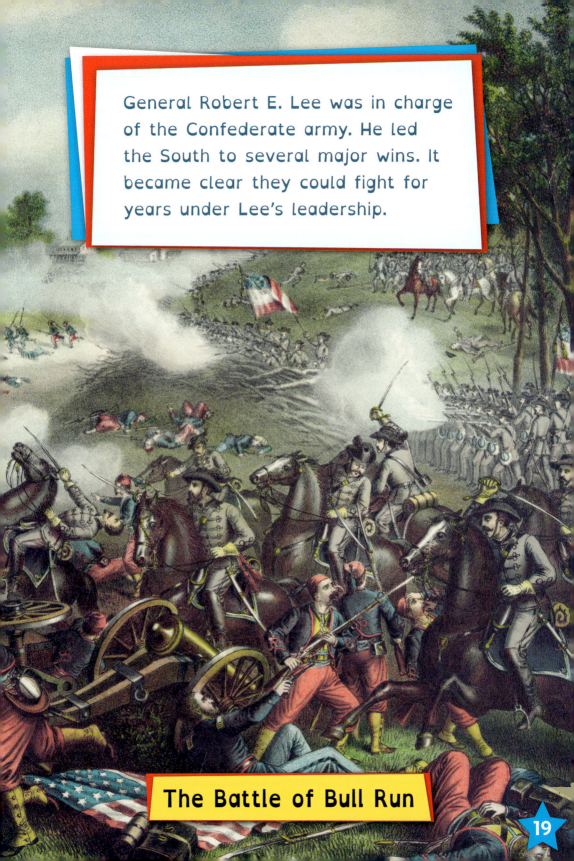

General Robert E. Lee was in charge of the Confederate army. He led the South to several major wins. It became clear they could fight for years under Lee's leadership.

The Battle of Bull Run

Slavery Ends

By the third year of the war, there was still no end in sight. Lincoln had to make a bold move. He decided to end slavery everywhere.

On January 1, 1863, he wrote the **Emancipation Proclamation**. It freed people who were enslaved in the Confederate States.

> This proclamation did something else. It allowed Black men to become soldiers. This was illegal before, even in the Union Army. Close to 200,000 Black men joined the war on the side of the North.

Northern Gains

In July 1863, the tide of the war began to change. The North started winning more and more battles. The South invaded the North at Gettysburg. Many soldiers died over three days of fighting. But in the end, the North won.

The Battle of Vicksburg was another important battle. It was fought around the same time. The Union win gave the North control of the Mississippi River. The river was used to send supplies for the war.

The South was losing on the battlefield. They also lost the fight over slavery. In January 1865, Congress officially changed the U.S. **Constitution**. Slavery was now illegal. In May 1865, the South **surrendered**. The North won the Civil War.

Lincoln did not see the end of the war. He was killed on April 14, 1865. Confederate John Wilkes Booth shot him at Ford's Theatre in Washington, D.C.

Robert E. Lee *(right)* surrendered to Union General Ulysses S. Grant *(left)*.

Trying to Unite

Tensions between the North and South continued after the war as the country tried to rebuild. Laws in some states made life hard for freed Black people. It would be almost 100 more years before Black Americans had equal legal rights with White people. In some ways, the struggle for equality is still happening today.

Laws that are no longer around have left a mark. Once, there were laws about where Black people could live. The laws have changed. But housing is often still divided to this day.

The Places of the Civil War

Review the states on opposite sides in the war and some key battle locations.

SilverTips for SUCCESS

★ SilverTips for REVIEW

Review what you've learned. Use the text to help you.

Define key terms

Confederate States of America
Emancipation Proclamation
secede
slavery
Union

Check for understanding

Explain how slavery was an issue that divided the states.

When and why did southern states secede?

How did the Emancipation Proclamation affect Black people in the country?

Think deeper

How do you think the Civil War affects life in America today?

★ SilverTips on TEST-TAKING

- **Make a study plan.** Ask your teacher what the test is going to cover. Then, set aside time to study a little bit every day.

- **Read all the questions carefully.** Be sure you know what is being asked.

- **Skip any questions** you don't know how to answer right away. Mark them and come back later if you have time.

Glossary

Confederate States of America a group of 11 states that separated from the United States beginning in 1860; often called the Confederacy

constitution a document with the basic laws and principles for governing

Emancipation Proclamation a document that freed Black people who had been enslaved in the United States, including in the Confederate States of America

forts strong buildings used during battles for protection

plantations large farms that grow crops such as cotton, tobacco, and sugarcane

secede to formally leave a group or country

slavery a system in which people are forced to work for no pay, usually under bad conditions

surrendered gave up on something, such as a war

tensions feelings of unhappiness and strain between two groups

Read More

Collison, Campbell. *The Presidents (X-Treme Facts: U.S. History).* Minneapolis: Bearport Publishing, 2021.

Gale, Ryan. *Fact and Fiction of the Civil War (Fact and Fiction of American History).* Minneapolis: Abdo Publishing, 2022.

Silva, Sadie. *The Civil War (U.S. History in Review).* Buffalo, NY: Enslow Publishing, 2023.

Learn More Online

1. Go to **www.factsurfer.com** or scan the QR code below.
2. Enter "**Civil War**" into the search box.
3. Click on the cover of this book to see a list of websites.

Index

Battle of Bull Run 18–19, 28

Confederate States of America 14–16, 19–20, 24, 28

constitution 24

Davis, Jefferson 14

Emancipation Proclamation 20

Fort Sumter 16–17, 28

Gettysburg 4–5, 22–23, 28

Grant, Ulysses S. 25

Lee, Robert E. 19, 25

Lincoln, Abraham 4–5, 12–14, 20, 24

plantation 8, 14

secede 12, 14

slavery 6, 8, 10, 12, 14, 20, 24

Vicksburg 22, 28

About the Author

Karen Latchana Kenney is an author in Minnetonka, Minnesota. She enjoys writing about equal rights for all people.